ARABESQ

A brief

The classical dance comes from Italy.

It was invented in the 15th century (between 1401 and 1500).

Then, it reached France, where it became famous thanks to Louis XIV.

Famous paintings by Edgar Degas

history...

As it happens, King Louis XIV was a dance enthusiast. In 1661, he created the Royal Academy of Dance, which later became the National Opera of Paris.

Thanks to Pierre Beauchamp, a dancer, and choreographer of the time, the terms of the classical dance repertoire were born.

French is used in all countries to refer to the technical terms of classical dance.
Some of the terms used are glissade, arabesque, grand jeté, attitude, pas de bourrée...

Ballerinas dance to classical music, most often played on the piano.

The music is counted in 8 beats. Sometimes, it is counted in 6 beats, also called the waltz beat.

The word ballet comes from the Italian "ballo", which means "to dance".

WARM-UPS

Essential to prepare the body for muscular, articular, and cardiac effort, they also help avoid injuries and improve performance.

They are done at the bar, on the floor, and sometimes in the middle (of the room).

Lifting

It is found during the "pas de deux": a moment during a ballet when two dancers perform a duet.

The tutu, emblematic costume of the classical dancer.

It includes the tutu itself, a skirt made of tulle, tarlatan, or muslin, and a low-cut leotard or corselet.

At the very beginning, the skirt went down to the top of the ankles, but it became shorter as the years went by.

THE TUTU IS TIED IN THE BACK WITH CLIPS OR LACING. THE DANCER CAN'T PUT ON THE TUTU BY HERSELF, EVEN DURING QUICK COSTUME CHANGES BETWEEN TWO ACTS OF A BALLET PERFORMANCE.

The learning of pointe is done after the age of 10, when the bones of the foot are well-formed. It is up to the teacher to authorize the beginning of pointe training or not. The teacher must ensure that the foot and leg muscles are strong enough to support the dancer.

The tips of the pointe shoes, made of reinforced cardboard and satin, are fragile. It is not uncommon for a ballerina to use several pointe shoes in one performance.

Most of the time, dancers have damaged feet.

Foot injuries are common because of how difficult the pointe technique is.

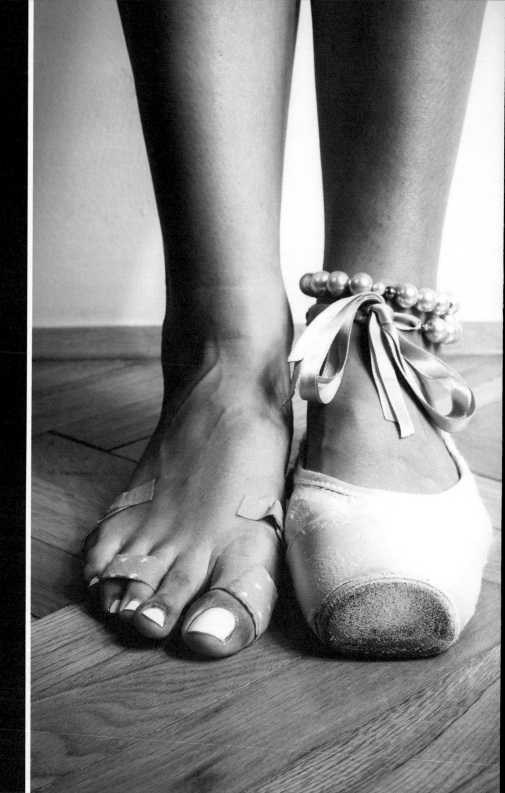

"Dance is the hidden language of the soul." Martha Graham.

Balance

GRACE

Resilience

Patience

Toughness

Hard Work

PERFECTION

Le cou-
de-pied

Flexibility

The title of "Étoile"
(star dancer) is given to
the best dancers.

It is the highest rank
known in ballet.

Star dancers perform the
leading roles in ballets.

It is awarded by
nomination at the end of
a performance and not by
competition like the other
ranks.

The other ranks
are :
quadrille,
coryphée,
sujet et
première
danseuse.

"To dance is like talking in silence. It says a lot without speaking a word."
Yuri Buenaventura

The freedom to dance

thank you
FOR Reading
this book

I hope you
enjoyed
Reading it as
much as I did
writing it.

Célia Milano

Printed in Great Britain
by Amazon

23245722R00023